IMAGES
of America

ST. LOUIS
IN THE CIVIL WAR

This is one of a series of patriotic postcards drawn by W.F. Burger in the early 1900s. Many were sent to commemorate Decoration Day. They are highly valued by collectors today. (Cher Petrovic.)

ON THE COVER:

The cover shows an encampment of the 1st Regiment, Missouri State Guard, only months before the tragic Camp Jackson Affair, a St. Louis mob action that ended in many deaths. This photograph was taken at the St. Louis fairgrounds in 1860. Col. A.R. Easton commanded the regiment. (Missouri History Museum, St. Louis.)

IMAGES
of America

St. Louis
in the Civil War

Dawn Dupler and Cher Petrovic

ARCADIA
PUBLISHING

Published by Arcadia Publishing
Charleston, South Carolina

Printed in the United States of America

Library of Congress Control Number: 2013942289

For all general information, please contact Arcadia Publishing:
Telephone 843-853-2070
Fax 843-853-0044
E-mail sales@arcadiapublishing.com
For customer service and orders:
Toll-Free 1-888-313-2665

Visit us on the Internet at www.arcadiapublishing.com

*Dawn Dupler dedicates the book with much love
to her talented daughter, Riley Luebbers.*

*Cher Petrovic dedicates the book to the memory of her great-great
grandfather, Private John Null, and all the others who fought for
what they believed in. May we never forget their sacrifices.*

CONTENTS

ACKNOWLEDGMENTS

Those kind enough to grant us use of images are credited in parentheses after captions. The authors wish to thank many people for their help during this project, including Pamela Sanfilippo, historian, Ulysses S. Grant National Historic Site; Janet Wilzbach, museum collections administrator, Jefferson Barracks Historic Site; Connie Nisinger, archivist, Bellefontaine Cemetery; Walt Busch, site supervisor, Fort Davidson Historic Site; Deborah Wood, museum curator, Wilson's Creek National Battlefield, part of the National Park Service; John Waide, St. Louis University archivist; and the Missouri Historical Museum. Additional thanks go to William Naeger, Tiffany Parker, Kate Worland, Joseph Maghe, Dennis W. Belcher, Randy McGuire, Lynne Martin, and Charles Orear. A special thanks to Dawn's husband, Michael Luebbers, for his editing and support. Also special thanks to Cher's husband, Bob Petrovic, for help with research and the use of his extensive collection of Civil War and GAR memorabilia.

INTRODUCTION

St. Louis's place in Civil War history is often overlooked, yet only Tennessee and Virginia claim more Civil War battles than Missouri. Politicians and generals recognized the city's importance. St. Louis was the eighth-largest US city in population at the time. It was key to river traffic, and the St. Louis Arsenal housed the largest store of weapons west of the Mississippi River. As war loomed, both the North and the South understood what the arsenal's firepower would mean to the Western theater should military conflict break out. The conventional thinking at the time was that whoever controlled the St. Louis Arsenal and its large cache of weapons controlled Missouri.

Having been settled by people from the South, the North, and by immigrants, St. Louis had a population reflecting that of the nation. When the secession crisis began, Union leaders worried that St. Louis could fall into Confederate hands. While Missouri had the distinction of being both a "slave state" and a border state belonging to the Union, many Missourians wished to remain neutral. Still, many supported the Confederacy. The City of St. Louis, with its influx of German immigrants, had many pro-Unionists who supported free labor. St. Louis became a crucible in which many different views on slavery and states' rights came together.

In the decade leading up to the Civil War, national attention focused on one enslaved man, Dred Scott, and his fight to become a free man. The Dred Scott case, first filed in St. Louis, made its way to the US Supreme Court, which ruled that Scott had no right to sue for his freedom, because Americans of African descent were not citizens. The court also ruled that the restrictions of slavery as outlined in the Missouri Compromise of 1820 were unconstitutional, throwing into question how and if slavery would expand throughout the United States, and in the process, contributing to the rising tensions between the North and South.

In May 1861, the annual Missouri State Militia encampment gathered at Lindell Grove on what is now the campus of St. Louis University. Pro-Southern militia members named the installation "Camp Jackson" in honor of Missouri governor Claiborne Jackson, a Southern sympathizer. Capt. Nathaniel Lyon, a staunch Unionist, heard of a plot by Confederates to ship contraband in the form of diverted US weapons to Camp Jackson so that the governor could seize the St. Louis Arsenal. In an effort to secure the arsenal, and in turn, the Union, Lyon led his army of 6,000-plus Union troops from the arsenal toward the state militia gathering to capture the encampment.

The militia at Camp Jackson found itself outnumbered ten to one and could only surrender. As Lyon's men marched their 600 captives through St. Louis, an angry crowd gathered. People jeered, some throwing rocks, then shots rang out. No one knows who fired first, but when the shooting stopped, 28 soldiers and civilians lay dead. The first military conflict in Missouri occurred in a clash between state militia and federal troops in what history would call "The Camp Jackson Affair."

The tragic Camp Jackson Affair came after years of tension between people who supported the South and its ideology and those who supported the North. Afterward, the state grew even more polarized into pro-South and pro-North camps. Men by the thousands joined either the Union or the Confederacy. For a short time in the city's history, St. Louis was home to two opposing armies. Only one could remain.

Recently promoted Gen. Nathaniel Lyon chased Governor Jackson and former Missouri governor Sterling Price, who both had declared allegiance to the South, out of St. Louis. Lyon battled Confederate general Price's troops at Wilson's Creek, where Lyon died, becoming the first Union general to fall in the war.

At the outset of war, Washington leaders called on St. Louis engineer and businessman James Eads to provide a solution to control the Western rivers. The self-educated Eads built the first ironclad gunboats to fight in the war, often using his own money to continue manufacturing around the clock. This new flotilla proved vital in capturing Forts Henry and Donelson and in opening the river for the Union army, leading the charge in the Mississippi River campaigns.

When war came, St. Louis was not prepared for the onslaught of wounded, sick, orphaned, and displaced. Jefferson Barracks, built to house and train troops, mustered in few soldiers during the war because the medical department turned it into an installation for the sick and wounded. Shortly after the war began, it became one of the largest hospital complexes in both the North and South.

Resourceful and charitable people went to great lengths to take care of those in need. St. Louis civic leaders Jessie Benton Fremont and the Rev. William Greenleaf Eliot organized the Western Sanitary Commission, along with the Ladies' Union Aid Society, which provided additional hospitals and staff. Steamships were transformed into floating medical centers. These two civic groups relied on private fundraising to operate. Hundreds of women left the parlor and provided aid, some risking their lives in the process.

During the Civil War, photography was in its infancy. Photographers could only take pictures of still objects. Due to the technological limits at the time—long exposure times and large glass plates required to capture images—most photographs taken during the war were studio portraits. The concept of the battle photographer had not yet been born. Scenes of battles had to be drawn or painted after the fact. This book presents some of those images and weaves St. Louis history through them.

The war brought tragedy to countless individuals. Before it ended, Missouri saw 27,000 of its own, both Confederate and Union, lose their lives. Some people gave their all for their beliefs. The story this book strives to tell is that of events and people in St. Louis, from well-known personalities that loom larger than life, to citizens who never would have expected their actions to be memorialized.

—Dawn Dupler
August 2013

One

ST. LOUIS BEFORE THE WAR
GROWING TENSIONS

In 1861, St. Louis was a Union-controlled city situated in a slave state with many Confederate sympathizers. The painting *The Last Sale of Slaves in St. Louis*, made around 1880 by Thomas Satterwhite Noble, depicts an enslaved family, reportedly the last to be auctioned off, on the courthouse steps on January 1, 1861. However, slave sales in Missouri continued until 1865, when emancipation for the state was proclaimed. (Missouri History Museum, St. Louis.)

In the decade preceding the Civil War, at least 30 slave traders were active in St. Louis. In the 1850s, Bernard M. Lynch owned one of the largest slave businesses in the city. By 1860, as the relative population of enslaved people dropped to around three percent, Lynch's slave business became one of the few remaining. Baptist minister Rev. Galusha Anderson wrote in his memoirs that on Sunday mornings, he saw from his pulpit Lynch's pen and witnessed "men and women, handcuffed and chained together . . . driven in there under the crack of the driver's whip." He further wrote about the squalid conditions he saw while touring its insides: "There was no floor but the bare earth . . . both men and women, herded together, without any arrangement for privacy." Thomas Easterly photographed this slave pen at 104 Locust Street. Lynch is thought to be among the men in this image. (Missouri History Museum, St. Louis.)

LYNCH, ARNOT & CO., liverystable, funeral and letting business, ns. Chesnut, b. 3d & 4th.

LYNCH B. M., dealer in slaves, 100 Locust; r. b. 4th and 5th.

LYNCH C. D., storage and com. mer., 271 and 273 n. Main.

LYNCH C. D., *(Wm. H. Keller & Co.,)* Barnum's Hotel.

LYNCH CHARLES J., grocer, c. Carondelet av. & Lynch st.

LYNCH DAVID D., grocer, n. 12th, b. Chesnut and Pine.

Lynch Dennis, stonemason, b. Morgan, Franklin av., n. 8th and 9th.

Lynch Ernst, slater, 11 Jefferson.

Lynch operated three facilities in St. Louis, one at 100 Locust Street, another at 104 Locust Street, and a larger site at Myrtle and Fifth Streets, which held enslaved children between the ages of five and sixteen years old. Auctions for the young were especially busy and difficult for abolitionists. Reverend Anderson recorded how he heard an auctioneer tout that one teenage slave had "the blood of a United States senator running in her veins." (Cher Petrovic.)

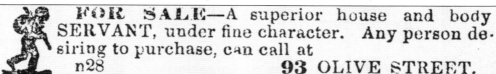

While the decreasing population of slaves reflected the declining importance and eventual demise of slavery, the buying, selling, and trading of enslaved people in St. Louis continued throughout the early 1860s, being legal until 1865. This advertisement from a St. Louis newspaper represents some common transactions of the times. (Cher Petrovic.)

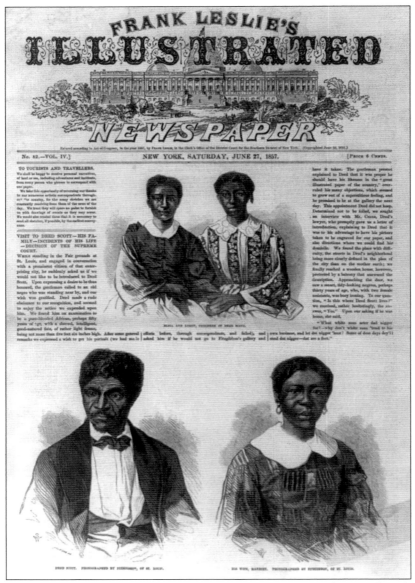

When army surgeon Dr. John Emerson died, his slave Dred Scott tried to purchase his family's freedom, but Emerson's widow refused. In April 1846, the Scotts filed separate petitions at the St. Louis Courthouse, claiming that they were rightfully free when Emerson had taken them to Illinois and the Wisconsin Territory, where slavery was illegal. What started as a straightforward lawsuit for freedom by Dred and Harriet Scott, filed by hundreds of enslaved individuals before them, turned into a series of court battles going all the way to the Supreme Court and resulting in a national ruling on slavery, wherein Scott lost his legal battle for freedom. This full-page article in *Frank Leslie's Illustrated Newspaper* of June 1857 depicts a familial image of the then-famous Dred Scott with his wife, Harriet, and two daughters, Eliza and Lizzie. The illustration helped to portray him as a person and not property. Nine months before Scott's death, his first owner's sons purchased him from Emerson's widow and granted him and his family their freedom. (Library of Congress, LC-USZ62-79305.)

The St. Louis Courthouse saw the first two trials for Dred Scott's freedom. When the Scotts lost their first case on a technicality, they attained a second trial. In January 1850, in a room situated on the courthouse's western side of the first floor, the Scotts won their freedom. But the politics of slavery were heating up, and their victory was short-lived. The case went to the Supreme Court, where the family's freedom was denied. (Cher Petrovic.)

When the nation learned the fate of St. Louis slave Dred Scott, outrage raced through the North, heightening tensions between Southern slaveholders and antislavery Northerners. The 1857 decision stated that Scott was not a citizen and had no right to sue because he was black. The Supreme Court also ruled that the restrictions of slavery as outlined in the Missouri Compromise of 1820 were unconstitutional. People could purchase copies of the ruling through advertisements, like the one shown here. (Library of Congress, LC-USZ62-132561.)

Chief Justice Roger B. Taney wrote the majority opinion for the Dred Scott decision. Declaring that all persons of African descent, free or enslaved, could never be citizens meant they had no standing in court. He lost much of his wealth during the war and died in 1864. (Library of Congress, LC-USZ62-107588.)

Abolitionist, Unitarian minister, and cofounder of Washington University William Greenleaf Eliot sought to influence politicians to keep Missouri in the Union and to abolish slavery. Eliot denounced slavery as "the most important problem of the nineteenth century." On several occasions, he personally bought slaves for the purpose of emancipating them. During the war, he was commissioner of the Western Sanitary Commission, an organization that helped the sick, wounded, and orphaned. (William Greenleaf Eliot Papers, University Archives, Department of Special Collections, Washington University Libraries.)

The St. Louis rivers facilitated trade, including the buying and selling of enslaved individuals. Most enslaved people lived and worked on large plantations in rural areas of Missouri, especially in the region along the Missouri River settled by farmers from Kentucky, Virginia, and Tennessee who brought with them a slave-dependent economy. These planters shipped hemp, tobacco, and cotton down the Missouri River to St. Louis. Many slaves were forced to work in St. Louis city, including those hired out to businesses. Many worked on the docks alongside free dockworkers, most of whom were German and Irish immigrants and most of whom opposed slavery. These 1858 photographs capture a busy St. Louis riverfront at a time when tension over slavery ran high. (Both, Cher Petrovic.)

Large numbers of Missourians flocked to the debates between Illinois senatorial candidates Abraham Lincoln, the challenger, and Sen. Stephen Douglas, the incumbent. What came to be known as the Lincoln-Douglas debates of 1858 focused primarily on the expansion of slavery into newly acquired territories. Douglas (below) was a proponent of popular sovereignty, which allowed for settlers to determine whether slavery should be allowed in their region. Lincoln (left) opposed this view and was against expanding slavery into new territories. He argued that the United States could not survive as a nation of half-slave and half-free states and spoke of the immorality of slavery. Newspapers across the nation sent reporters to cover the seven debates. Lincoln lost the senate bid to Douglas, but he would go on to win the presidential election in 1860. These photographs were taken in 1858. (Left, Library of Congress, LC-USZ62-16377; below, Library of Congress, LC-DIG-ppmsca-2679.)

This biting cartoon depicts Dred Scott playing the music to which all 1860 US presidential candidates had to dance. The slavery issue, represented by Scott, is editorialized as driving the election. All four candidates who sought the presidency are paired with people with whom the press identified them. Abraham Lincoln, nominee of the Republican Party, dances with an African American at upper right, while his rival in the North, Stephen Douglas, is shown at lower left with a Catholic immigrant. In the South, the race was between Southern Democrat John C. Breckinridge, seen at upper left with ally James Buchanan, and Constitutional Union Party candidate John Bell, at lower right with a Native American. Although Stephen Douglas won the state of Missouri, the city of St. Louis voted for Lincoln. With Lincoln's presidential victory, war appeared imminent. After Fort Sumter fell to the Confederates in April 1861, tensions in Missouri ran higher than ever. Lincoln called for the state to contribute 4,000 troops. To that request, pro-Southern Missouri governor Claiborne Fox Jackson publicly responded that such a requisition was "illegal, unconstitutional . . . and cannot be complied with." (Library of Congress, LC-USZ62-14827.)

THE OUTBREAK OF THE REBELLION IN THE UNITED STATES 1861.

After the war, New York printers Charles Kimmel and Thomas Forster sold hundreds of lithographs depicting popular patriotic themes. This 1866 print captures the sentiment at the onset of the war. Liberty wears a cap long associated with emancipated Roman slaves and stands on the shackles of slavery. President Buchanan sleeps while the Union is breaking apart, and a crowned snake twists around a South Carolina palmetto, spitting venom at Justice and Liberty. Secretary of War John B. Floyd scoops money into a bag, hinting at the allegations of his ill-gotten gains during office prior to joining the Confederacy. President Lincoln and Gen. Winfield Scott rally citizens to stand for the Union, while Confederate president Jefferson Davis, vice president Alexander Stephens, and their supporters tear down the US flag. Women and children weep for lost soldiers. (LOC, LC-DIG-pga-01777.)

Two

THE ST. LOUIS ARSENAL
THE PRIZE

Situated on a bluff overlooking the Mississippi River, the St. Louis Arsenal's location was chosen for its strategic position. The bluffs offered an ideal vantage point, and a natural outcropping of stone acted as a port where ships could be loaded and unloaded. Seen here is the three-story main building of the installation. (St. Louis University Archives.)

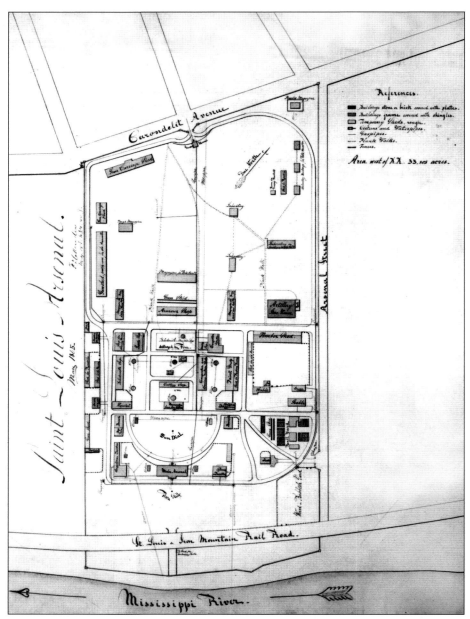

With 30-plus acres housing more than 20 buildings, and a railroad passing through, the arsenal was dedicated to supplying troops west of the Mississippi. The St. Louis Arsenal assembled small arms, rifle muskets, and artillery from components shipped from larger armories in Springfield, Massachusetts, and Harper's Ferry, Virginia. The arsenal manufactured ammunition, including the Minié ball, which came into prominence during the Civil War era. Only a few officers supervised the work performed by a local labor force comprised largely of German immigrants. With the arsenal's tens of thousands of rifle muskets and side arms and its ammunition stockpiles, the attention it received from both Union and Confederate supporters increased. The conventional thinking at the time was that whoever controlled the arsenal controlled Missouri. Shown here is an 1865 site plan of the arsenal. (St. Louis University Archives.)

Secretary of War John B. Floyd, former governor of Virginia, oversaw the distribution of arms. As hostilities grew, collecting arms became critical. Northerners accused Floyd of moving supplies from Northern to Southern arsenals. U.S. Grant wrote that Floyd "distributed the cannon and small arms from Northern arsenals throughout the South so as to be on hand when treason wanted them." When Virginia seceded, Floyd became a general in the Confederacy. (Library of Congress, LC-DIG-cwpbh-01731.)

West Point graduate Robert Anderson served at the St. Louis Arsenal in 1833 as a second lieutenant. Anderson is more famous for his role as the commander at Fort Sumter when it was attacked by Confederate forces in April 1861, making it the first battle of the Civil War. (Library of Congress, LC-DIG-cwpb-05635.)

Congressman Francis "Frank" Preston Blair teamed with Nathaniel Lyon to secure the St. Louis Arsenal. Popular with German Americans, Blair recruited many for service in the Home Guard, which supported the Union. He led his 1st US Volunteers in the capture of Camp Jackson. (St. Louis University Archives.)

Frank Blair lobbied to have the staunchly antislavery Capt. Nathaniel Lyon placed as commander of the arsenal because of their shared political views. Lyon, a West Point graduate, perceived in his superiors a lack of urgency when it came to securing the arsenal against an attack from those wanting its weapons for the Confederacy. Not long after coming to St. Louis, Lyon gained command of the arsenal. (St. Louis University Archives.)

With the fear that the arsenal would be attacked by pro-Southern troops, efforts continued to secure the installation and keep it under Union control. Capt. Thomas Sweeney positioned shooters along the building walls along with howitzers aimed at the arsenal gates. Sweeney would go on to become a general in the Union army. (Library of Congress, LC-DIG-cwpbh-03091.)

In April 1861, Missouri governor Claiborne Fox Jackson, a Southern sympathizer, refused to answer President Lincoln's call for troops after Fort Sumter fell to Confederate forces. "Not one man will the state of Missouri furnish to carry on any such unholy crusade," wrote Governor Jackson to Secretary of War Simon Cameron. (St. Louis University Archives.)

Apprehension increased as Lincoln called for men to protect the Union. In early 1861, St. Louis attorney and Kentucky native Basil Duke (left) recruited pro-secessionists into the ranks of the Minute Men, who later became the Missouri Militia. On the eve of the Missouri State Convention in St. Louis, whose agenda was to determine how to handle the secession issue, Duke and his men gathered at their Berthold Mansion headquarters (above). Here, men fashioned a secession flag and flew it over the building's front porch in an admittedly deliberate attempt to provoke the Wide Awakes, a pro-Union paramilitary club. Civic leaders intervened to prevent violence when the two groups were about to come to blows over the flying of the Confederate symbol. (Both, Cher Petrovic.)

After the attack on Fort Sumter and the Missouri governor's refusal to support the president, efforts to fortify the arsenal against an attack by pro-Southern forces were stepped up. This image from a war-era *Harper's* magazine titled "Fortifications Being Erected at the Arsenal, 1861" depicts just that. By this time, the facility held enough weapons to equip up to 50,000 men. By this time, tensions between pro-Confederate sympathizers and Union supporters continued to mount, and as war became imminent, this massive firepower grew more desirable to both sides. Capt. Nathaniel Lyon and Frank Blair gathered men to ramp up fortifications of the St. Louis Arsenal for fear that its vast amounts of munitions would fall into enemy hands. Men aimed rifles and howitzers at the arsenal gates that were most likely to be attacked. Munitions considered to be excess were transferred to storage in Alton, Illinois. While the small contingent of men at the arsenal remained ready, they were never assaulted. (St. Louis University Archives.)

Workers at the St. Louis Arsenal sorted and stacked tens of thousands of cannon balls. This stockpile of ammunition was stored in what was termed the "Ball Yard." Behind these can be seen stacks of cannon barrels. This photograph was taken in 1866, but it depicts how the arsenal was used during the war. (Missouri History Museum, St. Louis.)

This ordnance sergeant stands next to items stored at the arsenal that would have been typically issued to men. Soldiers carried water-resistant haversacks for personal items such as letters and books, canteens covered in blue wool, and wore a waist belt and a scabbard for a bayonet. A leather box held the twisted paper cartridges, containing both ball and powder, used as ammunition. Firing caps were kept in a separate pouch. (St. Louis University Archives.)

Three

CAMP JACKSON
A MOB ACTION

The tragic events on May 10, 1861, following the capture of the militia at Camp Jackson, have long been called "The Camp Jackson Affair." Prisoners captured at Camp Jackson were marched to the St. Louis Arsenal as a crowd gathered and grew angry. No one knows who fired the first shot, but after the volley of gunfire, no fewer than 28 civilians and soldiers were dead. Most consider these people Missouri's first Civil War casualties. (Library of Congress, LC-USZ62-132566.)

Gov. Claiborne Jackson called the legally sanctioned gathering of the Missouri State Volunteer Militia in May 1861. While most Missourians were considered pro-Union but not necessarily antislavery, Jackson led a powerful minority of pro-secessionists The annual militia muster, usually a festive reunion of men, began with some tension. Jackson, a Southern sympathizer, had defied President Lincoln's request for troops to help preserve the Union. (St. Louis University Archives.)

With secession sentiment heavy throughout the camp, soldiers named the gathering "Camp Jackson," after the governor, and named many streets after Confederate generals. Captain Lyon, already outraged that Governor Jackson refused Lincoln's call for troops, suspected Confederate arms had been moved to the camp and took it upon himself to surround the militia of 600-plus men with his force of over 6,000 troops. The camp surrendered, and the men were marched through St. Louis. They were forced to take a loyalty oath and were paroled. Today, St. Louis University stands on the area where these men encamped. (St. Louis University Archives.)

When Carl Juengel, seen here, was a 10-year-old boy, he asked his grandfather, Johannes Juengel, to take him to see the dress parade that the Camp Jackson soldiers had scheduled. According to Carl's diaries, written as an adult, he, his grandfather, grandmother, and uncle waited at the street. Rather than a dress parade, a captured militia marched past, and mob violence commenced. When the shooting stopped, his grandfather lay dead. (Kate Worland.)

William "Jeffery" Bull, seen here wearing his Camp Jackson uniform, including engineer corps insignia, enlisted in the 2nd National Guard, Missouri Volunteer Militia. The militia, faithful to Gov. Claiborne Jackson and the secessionists, surrendered to Federal troops. Maj. Gen. John C. Frémont directed that prisoners who signed loyalty oaths to the Union be paroled. The handwritten note on the back of this photograph reads that it was taken by J. Sidney one month before going south with other Camp Jackson prisoners who were exchanged for those taken captive by Gen. Sterling Price at Lexington, Missouri. Prisoner exchanges early in the war were primarily done out of necessity—neither side had adequate resources or places to house captives. Although paroled prisoners took an oath to not take up arms against the Union, many continued to fight for the Confederacy. (Missouri History Museum, St. Louis.)

Capt. Nathaniel Lyon, sure that Confederate weapons had been smuggled to Camp Jackson and confident that Governor Jackson planned to deliver the St. Louis Arsenal to the South, marched a force in excess of 6,000 men that took the militia encampment. Most of his troops were from the German community and were staunchly antislavery. (Library of Congress, LC-USZ62-35096.)

Brig. Gen. Daniel Frost, commander of Camp Jackson, proclaimed that his encampment was legal and that Captain Lyon's demand for his surrender constituted "an unwarranted attack." Outnumbered ten to one, Frost had no choice but to capitulate. Shortly after, he left the Union and became a brigadier general in the Confederate army. After the war, he returned to St. Louis. (Missouri History Museum, St. Louis.)

Ulysses S. Grant, future general of all Union armies and, later, US president, was visiting St. Louis the day of the Camp Jackson Affair. At the time, Grant was a civilian. He married a St. Louis woman, Julia Dent, and made several unsuccessful attempts as a businessman between his service during the Mexican War and the Civil War. He was visiting the arsenal when Blair left with his troops. (Library of Congress, LC-USZ62-1770.)

William Tecumseh Sherman, the Union general known for his scorched-earth warfare, lived in St. Louis at the time of the Camp Jackson conflict. The red-headed West Point graduate had resigned from the army and was working as president of the St. Louis Rail Car, a trolley company. He and his son Willie stood in the crowd as the captured Camp Jackson soldiers marched by. They dove into a ditch when the shooting started, escaping harm. (Library of Congress, LC-USZ62-112190.)

Prior to the events at Camp Jackson, former Missouri governor Sterling Price (right) viewed himself as a conditional Unionist—one who wanted the Union to remain intact yet still allow for slavery. After the capture at Camp Jackson, however, the Missouri State Guard was formed and Governor Jackson made Price commander of Missouri military forces. This made St. Louis the home of two opposing armies. Gen. William S. Harney (below), commander of the US Army's Western Department, tried to keep peace in an unsettled Missouri and keep the state in the Union by entering into an agreement with Price meant to suppress hostilities. On May 21, 1861, the two leaders struck a truce known as the Price-Harney Agreement. Shortly afterward, President Lincoln relieved Harney of his command and replaced him with recently promoted Brig. Gen. Nathaniel Lyon. Given Lyon's strong Unionist stance, the truce ended at this point. Price's Confederate army controlled southwest Missouri until the Battle of Pea Ridge in March 1862. (Right, Missouri History Museum, St. Louis; below, Library of Congress, LC-DIG-cwpb-04404.)

This Missouri State Guard encampment, held at the St. Louis fairgrounds in 1860 and dubbed Camp Lewis, is an example of the festive atmosphere these gatherings normally embodied. After serious marches and drills, socializing became a priority. The young drummer boy epitomizes the family connection to these events. Friends and family arrived in wagons and on foot to walk the streets of the camp and visit; picnic meals would be held, and stories would be swapped. People looked forward to the annual encampment and its festivities. (Missouri History Museum, St. Louis.)

Following the capture of Camp Jackson, the state was in turmoil. At the Planter's House Hotel (pictured), a site chosen because of its neutrality, Governor Jackson, Gen. Sterling Price, Brig. Gen. Nathaniel Lyon, and Gen. Frank Blair met for the purpose of reaching another truce. After several hours, the men knew that peace was impossible. Lyon's famous words from the meeting are attributed as, "This means war." After the failed meeting, Lyon and Blair headed out with troops to rid Jefferson City of Governor Jackson and other secessionists. (Cher Petrovic.)

On August 10, 1861, Brig. Gen. Nathaniel Lyon and his army fought Confederate troops near Springfield, Missouri, in what would be known as the Battle of Wilson's Creek. Lyon was killed and became the first Union general to perish in the war. This defeat for the Union gave the Confederates control of southwestern Missouri. (Library of Congress, LC-DIG-pga-01861.)

One of three German-born-and-raised major generals in the Civil War, Peter Joseph Osterhaus fled to the United States and settled in St. Louis after fighting in the German Revolution in 1848. As did most Germans, he sided with the Union. When war broke out, he led men in the 2nd Missouri Volunteers. In St. Louis, he commanded a brigade of riflemen during the capture of Camp Jackson. His soldiers were first on the field and last off at the Battle of Wilson's Creek. General Osterhaus fought in nearly every major battle in the Western theater. He was one of the last surviving Union major generals, dying in Germany during World War I. (Joseph Maghe.)

Benjamin McCulloch fought in the Texas army before war broke out in the United States. Appointed to brigadier general in the Confederate army, McCulloch used his troops to reinforce the Missouri State Guard southwest of Springfield, Missouri, and led the victory at the Battle of Wilson's Creek. He died the following year at the Battle of Pea Ridge in Arkansas. (Library of Congress, LC-DIG-cwpb-07505.)

German immigrant Franz Sigel directed the St. Louis public schools before accepting the commission of colonel of the 3rd Missouri Infantry. Sigel had served under Lyon during the capture at Camp Jackson. Afterward, he led a Union force headed for the capital that followed Lyon's troops. He achieved success, defeating Confederates at Boonville, Missouri, but later suffered defeat at Neosho, Missouri. He joined Lyon at Wilson's Creek. (Library of Congress, LC-DIG-cwpb-05088.)

West Point graduate and former Washington University professor John McAllister Schofield served as Nathaniel Lyon's chief of staff. During the Battle of Wilson's Creek, Schofield distinguished himself and became a Medal of Honor recipient. He would go on to serve under Sherman in his Atlanta campaign and later was US secretary of war. (Library of Congress, LC-DIG-cwpb-07122.)

The man seated on the left is Pvt. John Straw, 3rd Division Infantry, Missouri State Guard. Early in the war, soldiers for the Missouri State Guard organized in Jefferson City and fought alongside Confederate troops. Straw was wounded at the Battle of Wilson's Creek. The other man is unidentified. (Charles Orear.)

The Missouri State Guard was a Missouri force that fought for the Confederacy. Shown here are Thomas Duvall (left) and his brother William Duvall. They, along with their brother Henderson, fought at the Battle of Wilson's Creek in the Missouri State Guard. None of the brothers survived the war. (The National Park Service.)

Confederate soldiers, including those in the Missouri State Guard, often provided their own clothes to supplement their uniforms. In many cases, a soldier wore his own clothing into battle. Pvt. S.W. Stone (left) and Pvt. P.S. Alexander are pictured in their civilian clothing, which they likely wore into battle. Stone wears a sheathed Bowie knife and holds a musket. Alexander also sports a knife while supporting a rifle. (The National Park Service.)

The controversial figure John C. Frémont, explorer of the West, first Republican presidential candidate, and staunch abolitionist, headed the army's newly formed Department of the West in St. Louis. He was criticized for not sending appropriate reinforcements to Lyon as he chased Price and his troops into southern Missouri. When Union morale reached a low following General Lyon's death, Frémont issued martial law for the state of Missouri. On August 31, 1861, Fremont declared that slaves belonging to Missourians who fought against the Union would be freed. President Lincoln, learning of this through newspaper accounts, feared that this action would alienate other Union slaveholding states. He could not allow a general in the field to determine slave policy, and he could not accept Frémont's bold actions. Lincoln demanded publicly that Frémont change his proclamation. When the general refused, Lincoln dismissed him. (Library of Congress, LC-USZ62-35088.)

Major General Frémont visited his soldiers in the field on the southwestern edge of Jefferson City in an effort to boost both public and military morale. Rumors had spread that Sterling Price's troops were growing by large numbers and preparing to take Missouri. Frémont spent much of his energy recruiting his own troops and deflecting growing criticism for an ill-trained army and for Lyon's death at Wilson's Creek. (Library of Congress, LC-USZ62-107439.)

Four

JEFFERSON BARRACKS
SUPPLYING THE WEST

This 1840 bookplate is the earliest extant depiction of Jefferson Barracks, the westernmost army outpost at the time. Created by artist John Caspar Wild, known for his artwork of the Mississippi Valley and the West, this image features the parade grounds in the forefront. The hospital can be seen toward the back right. Like the St. Louis Arsenal, the barracks' location along the Mississippi River offered it a strategic advantage. (Jefferson Barracks Historic Site and Museum Collection.)

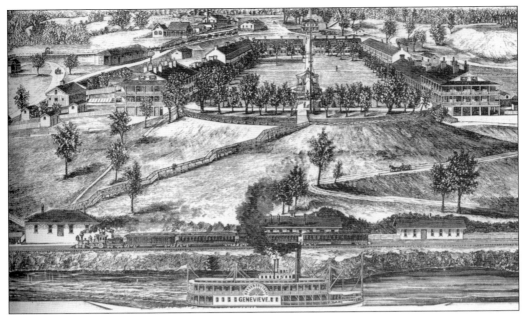

Jefferson Barracks functioned as the busiest military installation west of the Mississippi River at the time the Civil War began. The Mississippi River and a railroad at the bottom of the bluffs offered efficient transportation. No fewer than 220 Civil War generals passed through the barracks at some point in their careers. (Jefferson Barracks Historic Site Museum Collection.)

When additions were being made to the Jefferson Barracks complex in 1857, the builders from St. Louis first had to erect a place to live, because the commute to the city was too long to make daily. Workers constructed the Laborers' House (right) along with a separate kitchen (far left) and a stable (center). (Jefferson Barracks Historic Site and Museum Collection.)

The Mississippi River, rich with limestone deposits, allowed for an onsite quarry overlooking the river. The use of this limestone at the barracks dates as far back as the 1820s. Builders used mules to haul the large chunks of limestone to the barracks, as shown here. (Jefferson Barracks Historic Site and Museum Collection.)

The quarry, seen here today, is no longer active. It appears not so different now than it did 150 years ago. The lines in the rock, its scoring, are artifacts from quarrying performed decades ago. (Jefferson Barracks Historic Site and Museum Collection.)

These photographs show soldiers' barracks, both a single-story and a double-story building, during the Civil War era. The buildings were made of thick limestone from the onsite quarry and were then whitewashed. Wooden balconies lined the buildings. For the most part, Jefferson Barracks stopped being a basic training center during the war and was converted into a massive hospital complex, with a separate building reserved to house the hospital stewards. While some men still mustered in at the barracks, most new troops trained at Benton Barracks or Post St. Louis to the north. With so many men being treated at Jefferson Barracks, the inevitable need for a cemetery arose, and in 1863, the army established the Jefferson Barracks Post Cemetery, which eventually grew into Jefferson Barracks National Cemetery. (Jefferson Barracks Historic Site and Museum Collection.)

Jefferson Barracks General Hospital was one of the largest hospital complexes in both the North and South. It had as many as 3,000 beds (the average hospital held between 200 to 500 beds) and treated both Union soldiers and Confederate POWs. At times, the facility housed more wounded than any hospital in the nation. Mobile field hospitals were set up about a mile from where battles were expected. After treatment in the field, wagons or steamers would transport the wounded to the barracks facility. The sick were also treated at the barracks. The cemetery that was established on the complex grounds was the beginnings of Jefferson Barracks National Cemetery. These photographs show Jefferson Barracks hospital from different views. Below, a hospital steward is visible. (Jefferson Barracks Historic Site and Museum Collection.)

Erected in 1851 by St. Louis master builder Francis Quinette, the Old Ordnance Room was the first of two powder magazines built at Jefferson Barracks. The second structure was finished in 1857 and is now the Powder Magazine Museum at the barracks. Both stored munitions, such as 46-pound kegs of black powder, bullets, rifles, and cannons. The buildings' design ensured that any explosion would be self-contained— the arched, plaster ceilings (below) and three feet of bricks above it would fall down and smother the fire, leaving the magazine's four-foot walls intact. The wooden floors were built atop dirt. Should an accident occur, workers could quickly remove the rubble and restore the powder magazine. The buildings were situated away from the barracks for safety reasons. No explosions were documented during the war. (Cher Petrovic.)

The above photograph, taken a few years after the war, shows the gate to the Jefferson Barracks post commander's house. After the war, munitions were collected and stockpiled. The solid columns of the gate are Civil War cannons. Builders fashioned the fence's uprights from stockpiled musket and rifle barrels, complete with fixed bayonets. The below photograph shows the gate today. (Above, Jefferson Barracks Historic Site and Museum Collection; below, Cher Petrovic.)

These original iron gates once greeted troops entering the St. Louis Arsenal at Second and Arsenal Streets. When the Aeronautical Chart and Information Center, formerly Defense Mapping, took over the arsenal location, it gave the structure to Jefferson Barracks, where it stands today. (Cher Petrovic.)

Mrs. E. Butler Johnson drew this image of the chapel at Jefferson Barracks for a series of book excerpts by Col. John W. Emerson. He described the building as the "unique little chapel in which nearly all of the renowned warriors [of the Civil War] have worshipped." According to writings accompanying the drawing, the original photograph deteriorated and no longer exists. (Walt Busch, supervisor, Fort Davidson Historic Site.)

Ulysses S. Grant first served at Jefferson Barracks as brevet second lieutenant in the 4th US Infantry upon graduation from West Point in 1843. He served in the Mexican War and returned to civilian life in 1854 in St. Louis. He reentered the military when war broke out, serving in St. Louis as brigadier general of volunteers. He went on to lead the entire US Army. (Library of Congress, LC-USZ62-101396.)

Sherman first came to Jefferson Barracks in 1850 and left the military in 1853. In 1861, at the start of the war, Sherman lived in St. Louis. Although Grant and Sherman attended West Point concurrently and saw each other in St. Louis a few times before the war, they would not be considered friends until they fought together. (Library of Congress, LC-stereo-1s02871.)

A West Point graduate, 1st. Lt. Robert E. Lee came to Jefferson Barracks in 1837 and spent two years as an engineer, altering the flow of the Mississippi River so water would more easily reach docks on the Missouri side. When states began to secede, Gen. Winfield Scott offered Colonel Lee command of the Federal army. Lee turned down this offer. Virginia had seceded from the Union, so he joined the Confederacy. (Missouri History Museum, St. Louis.)

Before Jefferson Davis became president of the Confederate States of America, he served at Jefferson Barracks in the 1st Infantry for a few months. Later in his career, he became secretary of war under Pres. Franklin Pierce. While in this office, Davis negotiated to put a railroad through the St. Louis Arsenal and Jefferson Barracks. (Library of Congress, LC-DIG-ppmsca-23852.)

Five

Generals
and Citizen Soldiers
The Work of War

Here, Gen. Francis "Frank" Blair poses with his staff. From left to right are (first row) Brvt. Brig. Gen. A. Hickenlooper, Maj. Gen. Francis Preston Blair, and Maj. Charles Cadle; (second row) Capt. G.R. Steele, Capt. William Henley (29th Missouri Infantry), Maj. Phil Tompkins, and Lt. Col. D.T. Kirby (29th Missouri Infantry). (Library of Congress, LC-DIG-cwpbh-03137a.)

Robert E. Lee first came through St. Louis in 1837. He briefly commanded Jefferson Barracks in July and August 1855 before serving in the Mexican War under Winfield Scott. When the Civil War broke out, he turned down an offer to lead the US Army in order to be commander-in-chief of Virginia's military, which eventually became part of the Confederacy. Lee would surrender to Grant at Appomattox in 1865. (Library of Congress, LC-DIG-ppmsca-35446.)

Joseph E. Johnston, a Virginia native and 1829 West Point graduate, served at Jefferson Barracks after fighting in the Seminole and Mexican Wars. He rose to the rank of brigadier general and was quartermaster general of the army, coming to Jefferson Barracks in 1853. When he left the army to serve as a brigadier general in the Confederacy, Johnston became the highest-ranking officer to resign his commission for the South. (Library of Congress, LC-DIG-cwpb-06280.)

Maj. Gen. Don Carlos Buell first came to Jefferson Barracks shortly after graduating from West Point. He returned to the barracks after serving in the Seminole War in April 1843. By June 1843, Lieutenant Buell was arrested and court-martialed for repeatedly striking a disobedient private, James Humphrey, with a sword, severely wounding him. Buell was acquitted of charges. (Library of Congress, LC-USZ62-80741.)

Honoring the war dead was something people did all over the nation. General and Illinois congressman John Logan, as national commander of the fraternal organization Grand Army of the Republic, declared May 30, 1868, as a day of remembrance. Logan wrote that he hoped the observance would be "kept up from year to year, while a survivor of the war remains to honor the memory of his departed comrades." (Library of Congress, LC-DIG-cwpb-07018.)

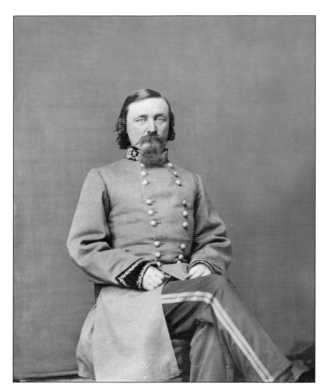

Graduating last in his class at West Point, George Edward Pickett went on to serve in the Mexican War with distinction. He came to Jefferson Barracks in August 1848 and remained there for five months before departing for duty in Texas. In 1861, Pickett resigned to join the Confederacy, where he would become a major general, best known for his futile charge at Gettysburg. (Library of Congress, LC-cwpbh-00682.)

Confederate general James Longstreet served as one of Robert E. Lee's top military leaders. Known for his fighting prowess at Second Bull Run, Antietam, and Fredericksburg, Longstreet is arguably most remembered for the Battle of Gettysburg. While with the Union, he served at Jefferson Barracks and became friends with Ulysses S. Grant. Historians agree that Longstreet attended Grant's wedding, but disagree whether he was a member of the wedding party. (Library of Congress, LC-USZ62-103595.)

Despite being outnumbered, Gen. Robert E. Lee defeated Maj. Gen. Joseph Hooker at the Battle of Chancellorsville in May 1863. Hooker's army helped secure victory for General Grant at the Battle of Chattanooga. Contrary to popular myths, the slang term "hooker" was in use decades prior to the Civil War; however, many historians write that Hooker's troops were often undisciplined and may have added to the term's usage. (Library of Congress, LC-DIG-ppmsca-19394.)

Philip Sheridan came to Jefferson Barracks, where he was appointed a captain in General Sherman's newly formed 13th Infantry. Promoted to major general in 1863, Sheridan's force battled Confederate cavalry at Yellow Tavern, killing Maj. Gen. J.E.B. Stuart. When Grant became president, Sheridan held many positions, including head of the Division of Missouri. When Sherman retired, Sheridan became commanding general of the army. (National Archives and Records Administration.)

Engineer Grenville Dodge was another general who came through Jefferson Barracks. Mustered into the army in July 1861, Dodge served as a major general and led men during the Atlanta campaign and, in 1865, commanded the Department of Missouri. Dodge recruited African Americans who had escaped slavery, forming the 1st Alabama Colored Infantry Regiment. After the war, he served in Congress and financed railroads. (National Archives and Records Administration.)

In November 1861, Henry Halleck, another general who had served at Jefferson Barracks, replaced John C. Frémont as commander of the Department of Missouri in St. Louis. Halleck issued an order, published in the St. Louis newspapers, that all Southern sympathizers must swear allegiance to the Union or pay fines. The following year, he fined citizens whom he considered sympathizers. Some people left the city as a result. (Library of Congress, LC-DIG-cwpb-06956.)

James Ewell Brown "Jeb" Stuart came to Jefferson Barracks in 1854 after graduating from West Point. He resigned his commission to join the Confederacy in 1861 and became a major general. Stuart fought at the Battle of Gettysburg, and was mortally wounded at the Battle of Yellow Tavern on May 11, 1864. (National Archives.)

Lt. Col. Gabriel Rains first came to Jefferson Barracks in 1848 as a captain of the 7th Infantry. He resigned his commission on July 31, 1861, to join the Confederacy, where he quickly rose to the rank of general. Rains led Confederate troops at the Battle of Wilson's Creek. He developed a type of field mine that was used in roads, causing many Union casualties. (Library of Congress, LC-DIG-cwpb-07530.)

Mansfield Lovell graduated from West Point and served with distinction in the Mexican War. He came to Jefferson Barracks in 1849 and became its commander the next year. He returned to civilian life, moving back to New York City in 1854. When the war began, Lovell joined the Confederate army, rising to major general. Lacking the men and weapons necessary to defend New Orleans, he made the unpopular decision to evacuate the city. (Library of Congress, LC-DIG-cwpb-06072.)

Another West Point graduate who came through Jefferson Barracks was Edmund Kirby Smith, who served in the Mexican-American War. Smith came to the barracks in 1848, served in Texas, then returned to a different assignment at the barracks. After war broke out, Smith joined the Confederacy and was severely injured at First Bull Run. He became a full general and commanded the Confederate Trans-Mississippi Department. (Library of Congress, LC-DIG-cwpb-06080.)

Cadmus Marcellus Wilcox came through Jefferson Barracks after graduating from West Point. He served in the Mexican-American War, fighting in many battles. He spent five years at West Point teaching military tactics, then arrived at Jefferson Barracks as a first lieutenant in the 7th Infantry in 1858. When war broke out between the states, he resigned his commission to join the Confederacy and was quickly promoted to general. He and his men fought at Chancellorsville, Salem Church, and Gettysburg, where his brigade supported the doomed Pickett's Charge. His postwar years included an appointment by Pres. Grover Cleveland as chief of the railroad division. (Library of Congress, LC-DIG-cwpb-06355.)

Samuel Ryan Curtis served in the Mexican War before becoming a congressman in 1856. When the Civil War broke out in 1861, Curtis resigned from Congress. In 1861, he was commanding officer of Jefferson Barracks for a short while before commanding the Army of the Southwest. Late in the war, Maj. Gen. Curtis defeated Sterling Price's forces near Kansas City at the Battle of Westport, one of the largest engagements west of the Mississippi River. (Library of Congress, LC-DIG-cwpb-06211.)

Montgomery Meigs served at Jefferson Barracks as an assistant to Robert E. Lee, working on navigation improvements on the Mississippi River. He put his engineering skills to use during the war, becoming quartermaster general of the army, ensuring that supplies reached the battlefields. (Library of Congress, LC-DIG-cwpbh-03111.)

When the Civil War began, Rufus Saxton commanded an artillery unit at the St. Louis Arsenal and was instrumental in moving soldiers captured at Camp Jackson to the arsenal. He moved up the ranks to brigadier general. While commander at Harper's Ferry, he earned the Medal of Honor for his service in May and June 1862. (Library of Congress, LC-DIG-cwpb-06589.)

Braxton Bragg had been to Jefferson Barracks several times before the Civil War, four times serving as commandant between 1849 and 1853. In 1856, he left the army to farm in Louisiana, but joined the Confederacy at the outbreak of war. General Bragg's service is wrought with controversy. While historians disagree as to his degree of culpability in defeats, they mostly agree that his military career was full of quarrels and bad decisions. (Library of Congress, LC-USZc4-7984.)

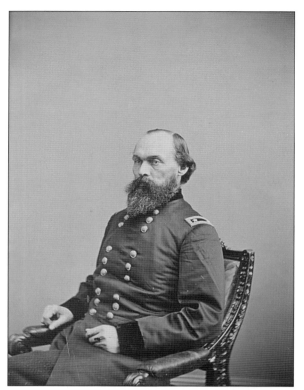

Gordon Granger came to Jefferson Barracks in July 1846. After distinguishing himself during the Mexican-American War, he fought at the Battles of Wilson's Creek and Island Number Ten. Major General Granger is associated with Juneteenth, the oldest known celebration of the end of slavery. On June 19, 1865, Granger and his regiment arrived in Galveston, Texas, announcing that the war was over and that slavery was abolished. Juneteenth commemorates that event. (National Archives.)

Winfield Scott Hancock came to Jefferson Barracks in 1848 with the 6th Infantry, served as regiment quartermaster, and moved up to assistant adjutant general before he left the barracks in 1855. He continued to serve the Union during the Civil War, earning the rank of general. During Gettysburg, Hancock received a serious leg wound fighting Pickett's Charge. In 1880, he was an unsuccessful nominee for US president. (Library of Congress, LC-USZ62-131810.)

Fitzhugh Lee, nephew of Robert E. Lee, came through Jefferson Barracks early in his career. Lee served in Texas before the war, and was a cavalry instructor at West Point when war broke out. He resigned to join the Confederacy. After the war, Lee rejoined the US Army when the country went to war with Spain. He was one of the three ex-Confederate generals to become major generals of US volunteers. (Library of Congress, LC-DIG-cwpbh-00683.)

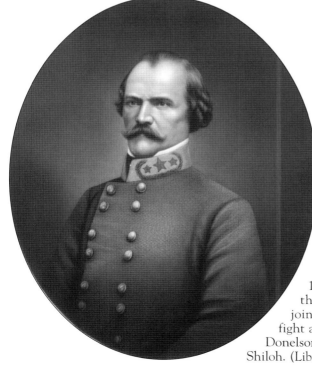

Albert Sidney Johnston served at Jefferson Barracks from 1827 to 1832, after which he left to serve in the Texas military. In May 1861, he joined the Confederacy and went on to fight at the Battles of Fort Henry and Fort Donelson. Johnston died during the Battle of Shiloh. (Library of Congress, LC-DIG-pga-04023.)

After the Mexican War, Irvin McDowell served as adjutant at Jefferson Barracks in 1852. Most historians agree that McDowell gained the rank of general because of his political connections. Having never previously led troops into combat, McDowell suffered defeat at the First Battle of Bull Run. During the Second Battle of Bull Run, he fared no better. For the remainder of the war, McDowell was inactive on the West Coast. (Library of Congress, LC-DIG-cwpb-05377.)

St. Louis businessman John McNeil spent his entire Civil War service in the state of Missouri. In 1862, McNeil was appointed commander of the City of St. Louis, where he was charged with clearing the city of Confederates. In October of that year, McNeil's actions earned him international notoriety; he ordered the execution of 10 Confederate prisoners as retaliation for the disappearance and presumed murder of a Union loyalist. (Library of Congress, LC-DIG-cwpb-05428.)

Seated third from left is Vermont native Joseph Mower, who joined the 11th Missouri Volunteer Infantry in May 1863 after having fought for the Union in New Madrid, Missouri. Earning the nickname "Fighting Joe," General Sherman said of him, "he's the boldest young officer we have." (Missouri History Museum, St. Louis.)

In August 1861, the 11th Missouri Volunteer Infantry organized in St. Louis and went on to distinguish itself in service. Among the battles and skirmishes in which it participated were the Battle of Pilot Knob; Ironton, Missouri; and Vicksburg, Mississippi. This soldier is identified as a member of the 11th; however, his name is not known. (Dennis W. Belcher.)

George Gould was a soldier in the 11th Missouri Volunteer Infantry, Company A. He was a farmer from Sumner, Illinois, before the war. In this photograph, Gould is wearing a shell jacket, which fit closer to the body, making it more practical for fighting. (Dennis W. Belcher.)

The 11th Missouri Volunteer Infantry was home to George Henry from 1861 to 1866. Before the war, Henry made his living as an attorney. After the war, he moved to Colorado and was elected to the state senate. He became a judge and died in 1907. (Dennis W. Belcher.)

At the beginning of the Civil War, attorney William Barnum joined the 11th Missouri Volunteer Infantry, at the age of 32. He organized a group of sharpshooters in Company I. When Barnum mustered out, he had achieved the rank of lieutenant colonel. He then moved to Chicago with his family. (Dennis W. Belcher.)

Pictured here is Eli Bowyer, MD, who entered the 11th Infantry as an assistant surgeon in 1861. Facing his own health difficulties, Bowyer still managed to serve the duration of the war and was promoted in 1863 to major and in 1865 to brevet brigadier general "for gallant and meritorious service." (Dennis W. Belcher.)

Edward King, of the 11th Infantry, served as a hospital steward. He helped the wounded after the Battle of Tupelo, which was fought in July 1864. In addition to injuries inflicted by Confederate forces, men suffered from heat stroke and other heat-related problems. (Dennis W. Belcher.)

Shown here are Capt. William Cleland (right) and Modesto Green. While few details are known of their particular service, it is known that most of the soldiers in the 11th Infantry came from Illinois, although the regiment represented Missouri. (Dennis W. Belcher.)

Records show that Wilford McElyea was a farmer before he enlisted at the age of 22. He served as a first lieutenant of Company F in the 11th Missouri Volunteer Infantry. (Dennis W. Belcher.)

James Lott earned his living as a carpenter before the Civil War. He enlisted in 1861. Although he was severely wounded in the Battle of Nashville in November 1864, he survived to be 80 years old. (Dennis W. Belcher.)

Col. Andrew J. Weber first tried to enlist when President Lincoln called for 75,000 volunteer troops in April 1861 following the bombardment of Fort Sumter. The call for men in his home state of Illinois had reached its quota, so he joined another company that became part of the 11th Missouri Infantry. A cannonball mortally wounded him at the siege of Vicksburg. (Dennis W. Belcher.)

While Samuel Moles and his Union garrison guarded a supply depot in Holly Springs, Mississippi, Confederate general Earl Van Dorn's troops made a surprising dawn raid on December 20, 1862. Moles and his fellow soldiers were captured. He was paroled shortly afterward and sent to St. Louis, where he entered civilian life as a store clerk. (Mike Fitzpatrick.)

German-born Adolphus Busch served as a corporal in Company E, 3rd Regiment Infantry, Missouri Volunteers. Busch is best known for cofounding the Anheuser-Busch brewery with his father-in-law, Eberhard Anheuser, who was a private in Company C of the Missouri Volunteers. (Missouri History Museum, St. Louis.)

Letters and newspaper stories document that many women joined fighting forces during the Civil War; their exact numbers, however, will never be known. Frances Clayton, whose last name was also reported as Clalin, is one of the more famous instances because of the photographs of her that exist today. Several accounts put her in the Missouri cavalry and artillery, having enlisted in 1861 along with her husband from Minnesota. She fought in the Battle of Fort Donelson in 1862. Her husband died in battle later that same year. She is reported as having received a gunshot wound in the hip, requiring hospitalization that resulted in her identity being discovered. Newspapers reported Clayton as being tall and proficient at swearing, drinking, and chewing tobacco, traits they attributed to her ability to pass as a man. (Left, Library of Congress, LC-DIG-ppmsca-30978; below, LC-DIG-ppmsca-30980.)

In late April 1861, the Caldwell Minute Men formed in Caldwell County, Missouri. Its company numbered 75 men and met in the town of Kingston, Missouri, for regular drills. As part of the Missouri State Guard, the unit fought for Gen. Sterling Price during his attempts to take Missouri for the Confederacy. The company became the Caldwell Light Infantry and left the county to head toward Lexington. In the photograph below is Capt. David Thompson of the Caldwell Minute Men, Company D. Shown at right is Felix Thompson of Company H. At the end of the Minute Men's service commitment, nearly all reenlisted into the Confederate army. (The National Park Service.)

The War Department allowed for African Americans to fight for the Union in August 1862. Any slave that fought for the United States would be freed, along with his family. About 8,000 African Americans fought in Missouri regiments. Benton Barracks housed runaway slaves, many of whom chose to fight. The barracks also mustered soldiers into the Colored Infantry. James E. Yeatman of the Western Sanitary Commission, however, reported that the treatment of soldiers of color was poor. Often, they were under-equipped and inadequately clothed, paid less than their white counterparts, and paid weeks late. Their living conditions were inferior compared to those of white soldiers. This was not corrected until June 1864, when Congress ordered equal pay, rations, and medical treatment for African American soldiers. Missouri was the first state to have African American soldiers in combat, at Island Mound, in October 1862. (Library of Congress, LC-DIG-ppmsca-36456.)

When the government turned Jefferson Barracks' primary function to that of a medical facility, Benton Barracks in North St. Louis assumed much of the operation of training soldiers who mustered in. In addition to white troops, both freedmen and fugitive slaves trained at Benton Barracks. The 2nd Wisconsin Cavalry is seen here in formation. (The National Park Service.)

White soldiers were commissioned officers over African American troops in the Colored Infantry. These two officers served in the 56th US Colored Infantry. In August 1863, Capt. Thomas Abel (left) resigned his commission in the Iowa cavalry as a clerk to come to St. Louis as a captain in Company B of the 56th. William O. Kretzinger came to St. Louis in September 1863 as a lieutenant. (The National Park Service.)

"Our Boy"

This carte-de-visite of Robert Walker was taken in the busy river city of Mound City, Illinois. As a crew member of a ship, his title was "First Class Boy," a position common for young sailors. Historians have estimated that at least 14 percent of crews on the river were African American. While many were fugitive slaves, many free people of color enlisted as well. Unlike in the army, African Americans were integrated into navy crews at the beginning of the Civil War and were paid the same wage as their white counterparts. A First Class Boy would be responsible for standing watch, delivering ammunition, and any other required task. This photograph is credited to Mound City, Illinois, photographer J.B. Leonard. (The National Park Service.)

Six

ULYSSES S. GRANT
WHITE HAVEN

The 850-acre White Haven plantation, situated west of St. Louis proper, was home to "Colonel" Frederick Dent, Ulysses S. Grant's future father-in-law. Dent's son roomed with Grant at West Point. While serving at Jefferson Barracks, Grant would visit White Haven, where he met Julia Dent, daughter of the colonel and his future wife. This 1860 image of White Haven's main house is its earliest known photograph. (Ulysses S. Grant Historic Site.)

Ulysses Grant and Julia Dent were engaged for four years and married after Grant served in the Mexican-American War. Julia became an army wife until Grant resigned from the military in 1854 and farmed White Haven alongside his father-in-law. They lived in White Haven's main house and Wish-ton-Wish, a home on the White Haven estate vacated by Julia's brother, who left for California. Grant spent a year and a half building Hardscrabble, the cabin home on the White Haven estate, but his family occupied it for only three months. After the death of Julia's mother, Grant's family moved back to the main house to help Colonel Dent. Grant had a hard time prospering in the civilian world, especially in the hard economy of the time. He moved his family to Galena, Illinois, but failed to do better there. In 1861, he reentered the military at the outbreak of war. (Library of Congress, LC-USZ62-128092.)

As on large Southern plantations at the time, Colonel Dent used enslaved labor to run the farm and the household. Meals were served by enslaved individuals, making it unnecessary for Julia to learn how to cook. The summer kitchen, shown here, stood separate from the main house and served as a place to prepare meals in the summertime so that heat from the stove would not enter the house. (Ulysses S. Grant Historic Site.)

When Grant, shown here, first arrived at Jefferson Barracks, he regularly visited the family of his West Point roommate, Fred Dent. Grant would often visit the Dent family farm, but his visits became almost a daily routine once he met Fred's sister Julia on her return home from finishing school. Grant wrote, "After that I do not know but my visits became more frequent; they certainly did become more enjoyable." (Library of Congress, LC-DIG-ppmsca-35555.)

Julia Boggs Dent, daughter of wealthy planter Col. Frederick Dent, was an educated woman, said to have been an accomplished equestrian and described as having a sparkling personality. She attended the Mauro Boarding School at Fifth and Market Streets in St. Louis. Initially, her father disapproved of her marrying a soldier, but he eventually relented. (Library of Congress, LC-USZ62-130774.)

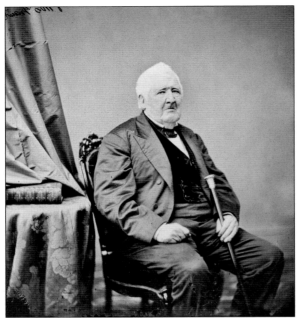

Col. Frederick Dent, the patriarch of the Dent family, owned 30 slaves. Dent showed support for the South by painting White Haven Confederate gray. When Grant came to own the property in 1876, he had the house painted Paris green, a popular color of the time. The circumstances under which Grant came to own one of Dent's slaves is unclear. Records show that Grant freed this person, William Jones, in 1859. (Ulysses S. Grant Historic Site.)

Julia Dent Grant lived and raised her children mostly at the White Haven home while Ulysses fought in the war. The couple had three sons (including Jesse, far right) and a daughter, Nellie (second from left). Often, Julia would visit Ulysses in the field. She was said to be a positive influence who buoyed his spirits. (Library of Congress, LC-DIG-cwwbph-04778.)

James Longstreet, future Confederate general who fought at Gettysburg and Grant's friend from his military academy days, attended Grant's wedding. Longstreet was also fourth cousin to Julia Dent. More than a decade before the war, the slavery issue was fiercely debated in America. Grant's family, antislavery Ohioans, were offended by Dent's enslavement of people, to the point that none of them attended the wedding of Grant and Julia Dent. (Library of Congress, LC-cwbp-06085.)

Colonel Dent enjoyed the trappings of success, which included a separate home in St. Louis. In August 1848, Grant married Julia at the Dents' St. Louis city home, located at Fourth and Cerre Streets. This 1934 photograph by Alexander Piaget shows the home. It had fallen into disrepair after the Dents owned it. (Library of Congress, LC-HABS, MO, 96-SALU, 2-1.)

When Ulysses S. Grant and Julia Dent married in 1848, Colonel Dent gave them 80 acres of the White Haven estate as a wedding present. In 1854, Grant, then a captain, resigned his military position and returned to St. Louis to build his first family home on the land. Before its completion, they lived at White Haven and, eventually, at Julia's brother's house, Wish-ton-Wish. Grant named his two-story, four-room cabin Hardscrabble, a moniker reflecting the building's rustic appearance, especially when compared to the grander White Haven and Wish-ton-Wish properties. The Grants lived there only three months. The above photograph shows Hardscrabble from the front. The below photograph shows the building from the back. Historians believe the bearded figure left of center to be Grant. (Ulysses S. Grant Historic Site.)

General Grant earned his nickname "Unconditional Surrender" at the Battle of Fort Donelson because of his statement, "No terms except unconditional and immediate surrender can be accepted." In April 1865, he accepted Gen. Robert E. Lee's surrender at Appomattox. These photographs of Grant and his staff were taken in October 1861. (Library of Congress, LC-USZ62-90934.)

In 1866, a monument was dedicated to the place where, in 1861, Grant received notice that he had been promoted to brigadier general of Federal volunteers, commanding Union forces in southeast Missouri. The monument stands on the lawn of Ste. Marie Du Lac Catholic Church in Ironton, Missouri. (Library of Congress, LC-D41-79.)

Ulysses S. Grant was commanding general of the US Army and, later, president of the United States for two terms. He ran as the Republican candidate in the 1868 presidential election. Although Grant's White House years were not without their troubles, he succeeded in bringing about legislation that furthered civil rights. His administration saw the passing of the 15th Amendment, which guaranteed the right to vote despite "color or previous condition of servitude," and the Naturalization Act of 1870, which allowed formerly enslaved individuals and their descendants to become citizens. (Library of Congress, LC-DIG-pga-00584.)

Seven

THE GUNBOATS
WINNING THE RIVERS

More naval encounters happened on the Mississippi River than anywhere else during the Civil War. Shipyards in Carondelet, Missouri, and Mound City, Illinois, built the first fleet of ironclad gunboats used in the war. This photograph depicts three of the US gunboats built by St. Louisan James Eads: the USS *DeKalb, Mound City,* and *Cincinnati.* (Library of Congress, LC-DIG-ppmsca-34028.)

Union supporter James Eads, a gunboat manufacturer, made his fortune as a young man by salvaging sunken riverboats along the Mississippi River. Eads, a self-educated engineer, devised his own diving bell from a 40-gallon whiskey keg, helping him reclaim abandoned cargo. By the time he was 40 years old, he had become a wealthy, prominent St. Louisan. (Missouri History Museum, St. Louis.)

Soon after war broke out, Eads expressed his concern about the Union's need for a strong navy presence on the Mississippi River to his friend, Attorney General Edward Bates. Bates, a fellow St. Louisan, knew of Eads's river expertise and supported his building a fleet. He also helped Eads get an audience with Lincoln. (Library of Congress, LC-DIG-cwpb-05606.)

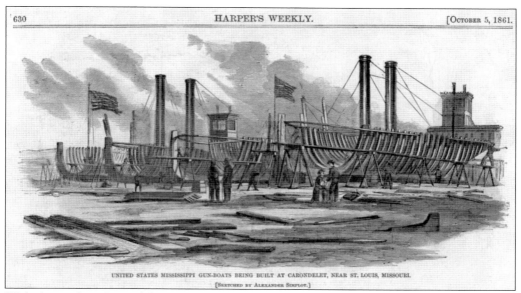

UNITED STATES MISSISSIPPI GUN-BOATS BEING BUILT AT CARONDELET, NEAR ST. LOUIS, MISSOURI.
[SKETCHED BY ALEXANDER SIMPLOT.]

With shipyards in Carondelet, Missouri, and Mound City, Illinois, Eads kept 4,000 men working around the clock, seven days a week. This *Harper's Weekly* drawing from October 5, 1861, shows his Carondelet shipyard. During disruptions in government cash flow, Eads financed construction with his own funds. (Missouri History Museum, St. Louis.)

After Eads traveled to Washington to meet with military leaders, the War Department contracted him for seven of what would be called "City Class" gunboats. These were the first ironclad warships to be built, four at the Carondelet shipyard and three at Mound City. (Missouri History Museum, St. Louis.)

In the first engagement of the ironclads in February 6, 1862, Andrew Foote used his flotilla to support Grant's attack on Fort Henry on the Tennessee River. As Grant's army advanced toward the fort, the gunboats fired. The fort surrendered before the infantry saw combat. Capturing Fort Henry along with Fort Donelson opened the Cumberland and Tennessee Rivers, allowing the Union to invade the South. This 1862 depiction shows the USS *St. Louis*, *Carondelet*, *Cincinnati*, and *Essex* capturing the fort. (Library of Congress, LC-DIG-pga-03975.)

In the beginning of the war, Confederates controlled what was known as Island Number Ten, a defensive position situated at a bend in the Mississippi River near New Madrid, Missouri. Commander Foote used his gunboats and mortar boats to lead an attack and shell Island Number Ten in April 1862. The USS *Carondelet*, *Pittsburgh*, *Cincinnati*, and *Mound City* played large roles in the battle. This print, "Bombardment of Island Number Ten in the Mississippi River, April 7, 1862," shows the three-week-long siege for the position. (Library of Congress, LC-USZ62-3115.)

Connecticut native Rear Adm. Andrew Foote worked closely with General Grant to take Forts Henry and Donelson, along with Island Number Ten on the Mississippi River. A staunch teetotaler, in 1862, Foote stopped the Navy tradition of issuing alcohol rations. As commander of the gunboat fleet, he came to St. Louis to inspect the shipbuilding at Eads's shipyard. He was injured during the attack on Fort Donelson and died of natural causes in 1863. (Library of Congress, LC-DIG-ppmsca-08352.)

Brig. Gen. Lloyd Tilghman battled General Grant on several occasions: Paducah, Kentucky; Fort Henry; and Vicksburg. After surrendering at Fort Henry, Tilghman was a prisoner of war at Boston's Fort Warren until he was part of a prisoner exchange. He then went on to meet Grant during his Vicksburg campaign and died at the Battle of Champion Hill. (Library of Congress, LC-USZ62-122975.)

Historians have documented that about one third of the USS *Cairo*'s crew were immigrants, largely Irish. On the *Cairo*, men from St. Louis fought alongside men from New York City and Boston. Records also show that as the gunboats traveled deeper into the South, runaway slaves joined the men. (Missouri History Museum, St. Louis.)

Naval commander John Rodgers and naval engineer Roger Pook set the specifications for the ships that would earn the nickname "Pook's Turtles." The shipyards built each ironclad to the same specifications: 175 feet in length and 50 feet in width. Manned by 160 sailors and officers and carrying 13 guns each, the ironclads became a formidable threat. Pictured here is the USS *Pittsburgh*. (Library of Congress, LC-DIG-ppmsca-34041.)

The Western flotilla played a large role in Grant's Mississippi River campaign. Seizing the river split the Confederacy in two. Although fought on water, the battles to take control of the Mississippi River were the purview of the army until October 1862. The navy provided the ironclads' officers, the army supplied the crew. Pictured here is the gunboat USS *Cincinnati*. (Library of Congress, LC-USZ62-65340.)

This is a photograph of the USS *St. Louis*. The first to be commissioned, it boasts being the first ironclad gunboat in the US military. Not long after its commission, its name was changed to the USS *Dekalb*, because the navy realized it already had a ship named "St. Louis." (Library of Congress, LC-USZ62-66706.)

Henry A. Walke commanded the USS *Carondelet*, leading the attack on Fort Donelson despite sustaining heavy damage. The boat also played a major role in capturing Island Number Ten on the Mississippi River. The *Carondelet* included four crewmen who won Medals of Honor, two for their actions during the Battles of Fort Henry and Fort Donelson. (Naval Historical Center.)

The USS *Mound City* fought in the Battles of Island Number Ten and Plum Point Bend, during which the boat was almost destroyed when rammed by the confederate vessel CSS *Earl Van Dorn*. The gunboat lost almost all of its crew when taking fire in St. Charles, Arkansas. (Naval Historical Center.)

The above drawing, "The Gun-Boat New Era," is from *Harper's Weekly*. The gunboat concept intrigued the nation. The first of James Eads's city gunboats was the USS *Carondelet,* launched on October 12, 1861, from the Carondelet, Missouri, shipyard. Days later, the USS *St. Louis, Louisville,* and *Pittsburgh* followed. From Mound City, Illinois, came USS *Cincinnati, Mound City,* and *Cairo.* The below photograph shows Eads's home, which reflects the wealth he amassed over his lifetime. Yet at the war's end he was far from done, embarking on new business ventures. (Above, Library of Congress, LC-USZ62-108449; below, Cher Petrovic.)

In addition to building 14 of the 22 ironclad gunboats used in the war, Eads accomplished one of the biggest engineering feats of his time: the Eads Bridge, which extended across the Mississippi River. After finishing his plans for the bridge in 1868, he saw its opening in 1874. The construction of the bridge used innovative building techniques and materials. In 1964, the Department of the Interior declared the bridge an official National Historic Landmark. This photograph shows the Eads Bridge during its early stages of construction. After Eads finished the bridge in 1876, he went on to develop a system of jetties used in the Lower Mississippi to keep the river navigable year-round. (Library of Congress, LC-USZ62-69757.)

Eight

HOSPITALS AND PRISONS
ST. LOUIS RESPONDS

Historians have estimated that for every man killed in battle in the Civil War, two more died of disease. Both sick and injured filled the hospital beds, most taking weeks or months to recover. The US Sanitary Commission was created by civilians and relied on charity groups such as the Ladies' Union Aid Society to give care and distribute items. (Library of Congress, LC-DIG-stereo-1s02810.)

St. Louis native Jessie Benton Frémont, wife of John C. Frémont and daughter of Sen. Thomas Hart Benton, worked with her husband to implement Rev. William Eliot's plan for a Western Sanitary Commission, a counterpart to the US Sanitary Commission. Created in September 1861, this important organization worked closely with the Ladies' Union Aid Society to give aid to sick and wounded soldiers and others in need. (Cher Petrovic.)

The Ladies' Union Aid Society was organized in St. Louis within a month of the Western Sanitary Commission. The organization solidified after close to 1,000 men wounded at the Battle of Wilson's Creek overwhelmed St. Louis medical facilities. At that time, many soldiers waited weeks in St. Louis, still in bloodied uniforms, before being treated. This print shows symbols of the era and women aiding soldiers and orphans. (Missouri History Museum.)

Activist and social reformer Dorothea Dix served the government as superintendent of US Army nurses throughout the war. She recruited nurses and obtained medical supplies from the public sector when none were available from the military. Dix came to St. Louis at the invitation of Jessie Frémont and met with the Rev. William Greenleaf Eliot, whose plan for a Western Sanitary Commission she endorsed. (Library of Congress, LC-USZ62-9797.)

The US Sanitary Commission fitted steamships with equipment and personnel to care for the sick and wounded. The commission also provided a fleet of transports—ships used to bring soldiers to St. Louis. At least a dozen steamers were turned into hospitals or transports. This drawing, "Arrival of the Twenty-second Indiana Volunteers," from *Harper's Weekly* of April 9, 1864, shows one such steamer, the *City of Alton*, docked at St. Louis. (Library of Congress, LC-USZ62-126965.)

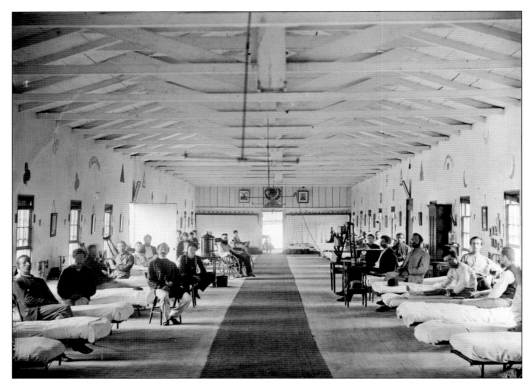

This unidentified ward represents the interior of a typical hospital during the war. Women were welcomed into hospitals as nurses and attendants in a way they would not have been accepted before. Many fugitive slaves, referred to as "contraband," worked for the Union. In 1863, the enslaved Anna Bradford Stokes of Tennessee escaped and worked aboard *Red Rover* as a nurse in the navy. (Library of Congress, LC-DIG-cwpb-04246.)

Early in the war, the need for hospitals grew urgent. The numbers of wounded astounded the St. Louis medical community. The US Sanitary Commission increased the number of hospitals in St. Louis to 15. Although the exact location of this St. Louis hospital is unidentified, historians know that the photograph was taken during the Civil War era, as the flag boasts 34 stars. (The National Park Service.)

While hospitalized for dysentery at Jefferson Barracks, Charles S. Eddy of the 18th Michigan Infantry wrote to his father in Illinois. His first letters were written in his own hand. As he lay suffering, the soldier grew so weak that an aide penned letters on his behalf. The letter shown here, written by Jefferson Barracks warden J.L. Cameron, informing his father of Charles's death, reads, "He was very anxious to see you and his mother and hoped to live until you arrived." Charles died while his father traveled to the barracks. The letter also expresses sympathy and includes "your boy's remains will be followed to the grave by the Ladies of the Sanitary Commission." (Jefferson Barracks Historic Site Museum Collection.)

In April 1862, the Union ironclad USS *Mound City* captured the confederate steamer *Red Rover* during the Battle of Island Number Ten in the Mississippi. The Union moved *Red Rover* to St. Louis, where she was fitted to be a hospital ship, complete with an operating room, laundry facilities, two separate kitchens for the sick and healthy, an elevator between the upper and lower decks, and supplies for three months. Commissioned on December 26, 1862, USS *Red Rover* became the first US Navy hospital ship. The Western Sanitary Commission contributed money and assisted in the conversion of the ship. Although the steamer was not the first floating medical facility, it was the first naval ship of its kind to be a fully fitted hospital with medical staff. In 1862 the first female nurses were assigned to the ship, transferred from Mound City, Illinois. (Library of Congress, LC-USZ62-97261.)

An illustration from *Harper's Weekly*, May 9, 1863, shows different scenes of the floating naval hospital USS *Red Rover*. In addition to a drawing of the boat, a scene labeled "The Sister" depicts one of the sisters of the Order of the Holy Cross who served as nurses. Other women functioned as nurses' aides and eventually as nurses. Some who traveled to battlefields by steamers to retrieve injured ended up suffering injuries themselves; Adeline Couzins received a bullet wound at Vicksburg while rescuing soldiers in need of urgent treatment. When the ironclad USS *Mound City* exploded during battle only one week after *Red Rover*'s commissioning, the steamer hospital moved downriver to take on the more than 100 wounded, many with extreme burns. Rather than simply transporting wounded to hospitals, *Red Rover* treated patients as would a brick-and-mortar hospital. (Library of Congress, LC-DIG-ppmsca-34030.)

Above, soldiers drilled moving soldiers on stretchers into a wagon ambulance headed for a field hospital. Below is a typical field hospital. Many Zouave units fought on both sides during the war, with at least 70 regiments active in the Union. Missouri had several such volunteer units, which distinguished themselves from conventional Union troops by their open-order formations, shooting stances, and double-time marching. Gen. Nathaniel Lyon supported the formation of the 8th Missouri Volunteer Infantry, a Zouave regiment that fought at the Battle of Fort Donelson. The French–North African jackets made the troops easy to recognize. (Above, Library of Congress, LC-DIG-cwpb-03950; below, LC-DIG-stereo-1s01796.)

This print from *Harper's Weekly* depicts women's new roles as nurses with the sanitary commission. In addition to nursing, sewing, and preparing meals, the Western Sanitary Commission and Ladies' Union Aid Society provided St. Louis women the opportunity to make an impact outside the home by participating in fundraisers. (Cher Petrovic.)

By 1862, many soldiers' children were orphaned or without a parent who could care for them. During that same year, the Western Sanitary Commission established the Soldiers' Orphans' Home, which cared for as many as 100 children at one time. This is a receipt for a $1 donation to the home, dated 1864. (Cher Petrovic.)

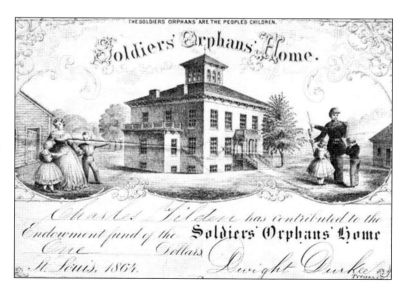

In need of housing for prisoners of war, the Union transformed McDowell's Medical College, founded by pro-Confederate Dr. Joseph McDowell, into Gratiot Street Prison in late 1861. Not only did it house Confederate prisoners of war and deserters, it also held those accused of being disloyal to the Union and individuals suspected of spying, women included. Federal authorities came into possession of the medical college when McDowell left St. Louis to join the Confederacy. The building was not designed for use as a prison; as a consequence, it was plagued by sanitation problems resulting in disease outbreaks. It was not intended to keep more than 1,000 people; at times during the war, Gratiot Street Prison held nearly twice that many. Executions did take place at the prison. Both sides retaliated against the other by executing POWs for a particularly offensive action. The prison stood on the northwest corner of Eighth and Gratiot Streets and operated until the end of the war. (Missouri History Museum, St. Louis.)

River pilot Absalom Grimes came from a Missouri family of split allegiance. While his brother fought for the Union army, Grimes earned a command as major in the Confederate army under Gen. Sterling Price. He also earned a reputation as an escape artist. When escaping en route to St. Louis's Myrtle Street Prison, the former slave pen, and on his way back to his unit, he gathered mail from Missouri families. On several occasions, Union soldiers captured Grimes, yet he escaped. In 1864, he found himself incarcerated in Gratiot Street Prison, waiting to be hanged as a spy. In an escape attempt, he was shot. He survived his wound and, through the intervention of a priest, had his sentence commuted. He lived to write his memoirs and died at the age of 76. (Missouri History Museum, St. Louis.)

A monument stands today in Jefferson Barracks Cemetery honoring the 56th US Colored Infantry. The inscription reads "To the Memory of 175 Non Com. Officers and Privates of the 56 US Infantry. Died of Cholera in August 1866." To the sides of this monument are markers for the unknown remains of this infantry. (Cher Petrovic.)

Outside of St. Louis, guerrilla raids turned many families into refugees. "Bushwackers" often drove people from their homes and took their valuables. While many raiders identified themselves as pro-Southern, Confederate leadership did not condone their actions. Refugees poured into St. Louis as people became homeless from the misfortunes of war. General Ewing's controversial Order Number 11 evicted most residents from four western Missouri counties as retaliation for Confederate raids. This action created hundreds of refugees. (Library of Congress, LC-USZ62-132937.)

Nine

FORT DAVIDSON
SAVING ST. LOUIS

When a Confederate soldier shot and killed a Union soldier in front of the Iron County courthouse, a few miles south of Fort Davidson, a group of soldiers returned fire from within the courthouse walls. Additional skirmishes took place the next day. Scars from stray bullets mark it today. In this photograph, soldiers guard the courthouse. (Walt Busch, supervisor, Fort Davidson Historic Site.)

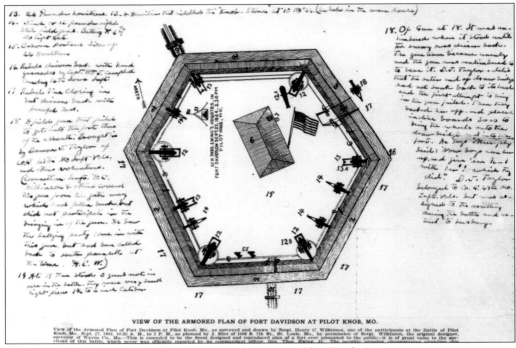

VIEW OF THE ARMORED PLAN OF FORT DAVIDSON AT PILOT KNOB, MO.

View of the Armored Plan of Fort Davidson at Pilot Knob, Mo., as surveyed and drawn by Sergt. Henry C. Wilkinson, one of the participants at the Battle of Pilot Knob, Mo. Sept. 27, 1864, 10:25 A. M. to 2 P. M., as photoed by J. Siler of 1006 S. 7th St. St. Louis, Mo., by permission of Sergt. Wilkinson, the original designer, surveyor of Wayne Co., Mo.—This is conceded to be the finest designed and reproduced plan of a fort ever presented to the public—it is of great value to the survivors of this battle, which never was officially reported by its commander officer, Gen. Thos. Ewing, Jr. The peculiar grossing circumstance standing this

Union soldiers built the earthen Fort Davidson, near Pilot Knob, Missouri, to protect against guerrilla raids. The fort was made of six earthen sides nine feet high, making a hexagonal mound fortress. Around it lay a dry moat, ten feet wide by six feet deep. In the days before Price's attack, civilians offered their help to defend the Union stronghold, many of them African American. (Walt Busch, supervisor, Fort Davidson Historic Site.)

William B. Rosecranz commanded the Department of Missouri in 1864. In St. Louis, with only 6,000 troops at his disposal to defend the city, Rosecranz learned of Confederate general Price's advance into south central Missouri. Needing to protect the only fortification between Price and St. Louis, Rosecranz sent Gen. Thomas Ewing with a detachment of 1,000 men to the earthen Fort Davidson. (Library of Congress, LC-DIG-cwpb-06052.)

2054

General and St. Louis District commander Thomas Ewing is credited with saving Fort Davidson and, arguably, St. Louis. At the start of his Missouri raids, General Price's objective was to take St. Louis for the Confederacy. On his way, he could not pass up the opportunity to take Fort Davidson and its supply of ammunition. Although Ewing's soldiers held the fort against three assaults, inflicting great casualties, he knew his men were greatly outnumbered and could not maintain their position. Ewing devised a plan to sneak his troops and all the ammunition they could carry, including six wheeled guns, past two Confederate encampments where Price's troops had regrouped. Before leaving, soldiers placed the ammunition they could not take into the powder magazine. Once the column of troops had safely escaped, the squad that stayed behind exploded the powder magazine. With no additional weapons and over 1,200 men lost in the earlier assaults, Price abandoned his plan to attack St. Louis. Were it not for the events at Fort Davidson, St. Louis may have been invaded by Confederate troops. (Library of Congress, LC-DIG-cwpb-06174.)

An arrow points to the hexagonal earthen Fort Davidson. The town of Pilot Knob is in the foreground, and mountains stand behind it to the left and right. In this depiction of the Confederate charge, troops can be seen lining up in columns before attacking the fort. Today, a large hole exists where the powder magazine exploded. (Walt Busch, supervisor, Fort Davidson Historic Site.)

Missouri governor Claiborne F. Jackson appointed his nephew John Sappington Marmaduke as colonel in the Missouri Militia. Marmaduke encountered Nathaniel Lyon at the skirmish in Booneville, Missouri, where Lyon's men defeated the militia in June 1861, only months before Lyon died at Wilson's Creek. The swiftness with which Marmaduke's men retreated became known as the "Boonville Races," embarrassing him to the point that he resigned his commission. Marmaduke joined the Confederacy in Virginia, rose to general, and came back to invade Missouri during Gen. Sterling Price's raids. He led troops at the Battle of Pilot Knob, where Price's troops were turned away from St. Louis. Marmaduke was captured in 1864 in Kansas and released at war's end. He settled in St. Louis and was elected governor of Missouri in 1884. (Library of Congress, LC-DIG-cwpb-06001.)

The charismatic Joseph Shelby recruited men for the Confederacy after the Camp Jackson Affair angered him to the point of action. As Price's men approached Fort Davidson for the Battle of Pilot Knob, Shelby rounded up more than 3,000 deserters, forcing them into his army. Some estimate that as many as one third of Price's raiders were deserters. Shelby's men were known as the "Iron Brigade" and gained notoriety for their raids throughout Missouri. At war's end, Brigadier General Shelby and his men escaped to Mexico. He returned to the United States in 1892, having received an appointment as US marshal of the Western District of Missouri. (The National Park Service.)

Louisa Volker became the first female telegraph operator west of the Mississippi River to serve in the US Military Telegraph Corps. Being the only operator available at Mineral Point, an important junction for the St. Louis & Iron Mountain Railroad, Volker sent telegraphs around the clock for two days straight when word of General Price's invasion into Missouri spread. Throughout the war, she sent vital military information. (William Naeger and Tiffany Parker.)

Irish-born Thomas Hanlon Macklind, an attorney and engineer, met Louisa Volker during the war. Along with other pro-Union men, he organized the 12th Missouri Cavalry. In May 1865, he and Louisa were married in St. Louis, where they lived and started a family. Years later, at age 58, Louisa graduated from medical school in St. Louis. (William Naeger and Tiffany Parker.)

Ten

ST. LOUIS CEMETERIES
THE BURIED, THE LEGACY

On February 21, 1891, a funeral procession of 12,000 soldiers and dignitaries, including both Union and Confederate veterans, marched seven miles to Calvary Cemetery to bury William Tecumseh Sherman. A caisson pulled his casket, draped in the US flag. This photograph shows the procession at Pine Street and Grand Avenue. (Missouri History Museum, St. Louis.)

Sherman owned houses in both New York and St. Louis in his years after the war. He continued to serve, becoming commanding general of the US Army in 1869. He refused to run for the presidency, saying, "If nominated I will not run; if elected I will not serve." This is a portrait of Sherman in his later years. (Library of Congress, LC-USZ62-72801.)

General Sherman's son, Jesuit Rev. Thomas Sherman, officiated at his graveside. Thomas received his law degree from Washington University, but he practiced law for only a short time before joining the priesthood, much to the disappointment of his father. Also present at General Sherman's graveside as a pallbearer was Confederate general Joseph E. Johnston. (Cher Petrovic.)

Not far from the Sherman family plot lies the final resting place of CSA general Daniel Frost and his family. Frost's grave is second from the left. A small Confederate flag lies atop his ledger. (Cher Petrovic.)

Dred Scott was first buried in the Wesleyan Cemetery, now the site of St. Louis University. When the cemetery closed in 1867, Taylor Blow had Scott's body reburied at Calvary Cemetery. No headstone marked his grave until 1957, the 100th anniversary of the Dred Scott decision. To the right of his monument is a marker for his wife, Harriet, who is buried in Greenwood Cemetery in north St. Louis County. (Cher Petrovic.)

Henry Taylor Blow and his brother Taylor Blow, children of Scott's first owner, and members of their extended family, helped to support the Dred Scott family during their years of fighting for their freedom. When Scott lost his court battle, he was legally the property of Irene Emerson. By then, the widowed Emerson had remarried Calvin Chaffee, an abolitionist in the US Congress. Amid accusations of hypocrisy, Chaffee arranged for Scott to be turned over to the Blow family, who freed the Scotts on May 26, 1857, in the St. Louis Courthouse. Scott's freedom made national news and brought unwanted attention, as he and his family lived a quiet life in St. Louis. Scott worked as a porter for Barnum's Hotel. Henry Taylor Blow served in Congress and also as an ambassador to Venezuela and Brazil. Taylor Blow was a St. Louis businessman. (Left, Connie Nisinger; below, Cher Petrovic.)

Francis "Frank" P. Blair Jr., congressman, senator, and general, is one of many notables buried in Bellefontaine Cemetery. On his passing, flags flew at half-staff and hundreds came by his house on Chestnut Street. Bellefontaine Cemetery was established in 1849 and is located next to Calvary Cemetery. (Connie Nisinger.)

Adolphus Busch served 14 months in the Union army during the war. At the time of his death in 1913, the wealthy entrepreneur's estate was the largest the state had probated. His memorial at Bellefontaine reflects the grandeur and status for which he was known. (Cher Petrovic.)

Don Carlos Buell served in the Seminole War, the Mexican War, and the Civil War. He led Union armies at the battles of Shiloh and Perryville. He was relieved of his command in 1864 for not having followed Confederate forces back to Tennessee. Buell spent the rest of his career as president of a mining company and as a government pension officer. (Connie Nisinger.)

Sterling Price served as governor of Missouri before entering the Civil War. While presiding over the Missouri State Convention, he voted for Missouri to stay in the Union. After the tragedy at Camp Jackson, however, Price led troops in an effort to secure the state for the Confederacy. He fled to Mexico after the war, but soon returned to St. Louis. (Cher Petrovic.)

James Eads had amassed his fortune before the Civil War began. After the war, he designed and managed the construction of a bridge across the Mississippi that was nothing short of an engineering marvel. Work performed early in his career using his own diving bell invention likely contributed to his poor health. (Connie Nisinger.)

Attorney general Edward Bates was the first presidential cabinet member to come from west of the Mississippi River, serving under President Lincoln. After the war, Bates was vice president of the Missouri Historical Society. (Connie Nisinger.)

Pvts. Fitz Guerin and Joseph Pesch and Sgt. Henry Hammel, all of Battalion A, 1st Missouri Light Artillery, took the initiative to man the guns and sustain the position aboard the steamer USS *Cheeseman* while taking heavy fire. For this action, all three were awarded the Medal of Honor. They are three of seven recipients buried at Bellefontaine Cemetery. (Connie Nisinger.)

Cpl. Lorenzo D. Immel of the 2nd US Artillery was awarded the Medal of Honor for his actions at the Battle of Wilson's Creek. New York Infantry private Martin Schubert received his Medal of Honor for picking up the 26th New York's flag during the Battle of Fredericksburg, carrying it until he was wounded. Both graves are at Jefferson Barracks National Cemetery. (Cher Petrovic.)

The 39th Illinois Volunteers color sergeant Henry M. Day's epitaph reads, "Medal of Honor for planting the colors on Ft. Gregg between two contending armies, April 2, 1865." Day was struck by a projectile when planting the flag. Historians report that Day's medal is in question because not all records confirm that he was a recipient; however, written accounts do support his bravery during the battle. Day was laid to rest at Jefferson Barracks National Cemetery. (Cher Petrovic.)

In 1866, Dr. Benjamin Franklin Stephenson founded the veterans' organization The Grand Army of the Republic (GAR) in Decatur, Illinois. All men who had served in the Union military were eligible for membership. In addition to being a fraternal organization, the GAR was a political organization whose purpose was to raise awareness of veterans' issues such as employment and pensions. Members wore a unique badge with a bar across the top bearing a bronze eagle and cannon linked by a ribbon to a bronze star. The bronze used in the badges came from enemy ordnance that Union arsenals collected after the war and melted down. In 1869, the eagle on the badge was redesigned so that the badge did not too closely resemble the US Medal of Honor. (Library of Congress, LC-DIG-pga-02757.)

The annual Grand Army of the Republic National Encampment was held at St. Louis in 1887. This arch was part of the ceremony. All officers and members passed under the structure during the grand parade downtown. City parks turned into tent cities as visitors flooded St. Louis. Many families opened their homes to out-of-town veterans and their families attending the encampment. (Cher Petrovic.)

During the GAR national encampment in St. Louis, this stained-glass window depicting Gen. Ulysses S. Grant hung from a downtown street corner and was illuminated by electric light. The City of St. Louis commissioned four stained-glass windows to decorate the city: two of Grant and two of Lincoln. After the encampment, the windows were donated to soldiers' homes throughout the United States. (Cher Petrovic.)

Shown here are souvenir items from the 1887 St. Louis GAR encampment. These items include various program books, a banquet menu, assorted medals, and delegate ribbons. The ribbon at the lower right is for the Woman's Relief Corps, the auxiliary to the Grand Army of the Republic. (Cher Petrovic.)

Shown here are 1887 medals. The upper left medal is a limited edition commemorative of John A. Logan, who died in December 1886. The ornament at the medal's end is silver. The center medal was given to all delegates and shows the GAR commander-in-chief, Lucius Fairchild. The other two were souvenirs given out by various delegations. (Cher Petrovic.)

The Grand Army of the Republic had many posts throughout the St. Louis area. Shown here are members of the D.N. Keeler Post No. 52 of Wildwood, Missouri, named after Pvt. Daniel N. Keeler of the 8th Missouri, who mustered out at Jefferson Barracks. The members of this GAR post met in a room on the second floor of the Kreinkamp General Store. Posts were named after officers, fallen comrades, and respected soldiers. Many were named after Grant and Sherman. (Lynne Martin.)

Both Union and Confederate armies hosted troop reunions in addition to the Grand Army of the Republic. Following the war, thousands attended as a way to commemorate the sacrifices made and to celebrate the friendships forged. The last annual encampment of the GAR took place in 1949. The United Confederate Veterans gathered for reunions also, as did groups of Northern and Southern soldiers together. Historians believe this photograph is of a reunion of both sides at Wilson's Creek in August 1897. (The National Park Service.)

Shown here are two patriotic postcards drawn by W.F. Burger, a popular artist of his day, and among the many produced by printing companies in the early 1900s. Civil War–themed cards commemorating Decoration Day and Memorial Day are highly sought by collectors. These types of postcards were often sent for birthdays and even for a patriotic Christmas or birthday. (Cher Petrovic.)

BIBLIOGRAPHY

Anderson, Galusha. *A Border City in the Civil War*. Boston: Little, Brown and Company, 1908.

Belcher, Dennis W. *The 11th Missouri Volunteer Infantry*. Jefferson, NC: McFarland, 2011.

Castel, Albert B. *Civil War Kansas: Reaping the Whirlwind*. Lawrence, KS: University Press of Kansas, 1997.

Erwin, James W. *Guerrillas in Civil War Missouri*. Charleston, SC: The History Press, 2012.

Gerteis, Louis S. *Civil War St. Louis*. Lawrence, KS: University Press of Kansas, 2001.

Grant, Ulysses S. *Personal Memoirs of U.S. Grant*. New York: Webster, 1885 and 1886. James M. McPherson, ed. New York: Penguin Books, 1999.

Lause, Mark A. *Price's Lost Campaign: The 1864 Invasion of Missouri*. Columbia, MO: University of Missouri, 2011.

Ross, Ishbel. *The General's Wife*. New York: Dodd, Mead & Company, 1959.

Speer, Lonnie R. *Portals to Hell: Military Prisons of the Civil War*. Lincoln, NE: University of Nebraska Press, 2005.

Straubing, Harold Elk. *In Hospital and Camp: The Civil War through the Eyes of Its Doctors and Nurses*. Harrisburg, PA: Stackpole Books, 1993.

Winter, William C. *The Civil War in St. Louis: A Guided Tour*. St. Louis: Missouri Historical Society Press, 1994.

Discover Thousands of Local History Books Featuring Millions of Vintage Images

Arcadia Publishing, the leading local history publisher in the United States, is committed to making history accessible and meaningful through publishing books that celebrate and preserve the heritage of America's people and places.

Find more books like this at
www.arcadiapublishing.com

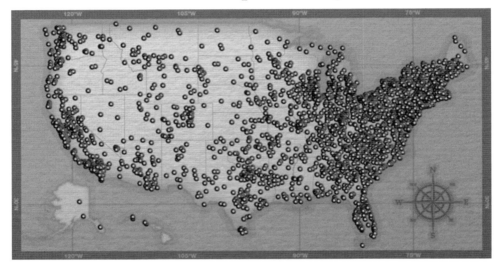

Search for your hometown history, your old stomping grounds, and even your favorite sports team.